MY FIRST
1000 WORDS

Consultant: Susan A. Miller, Ed.D.

Picture credits: Adobe Systems, Inc.; Amana; Aquaware America; Artville; Brand X Pictures; Brian Warling Studios; Comstock; Cuisinart; Farberware; General Electric; Getty Images; Image Club; Kolcraft; Anna Lender; Brian Meyer; Nicholas Myers; James Mravec; Julie Risko Neely; Rachel Perrine; PhotoDisc; Rebecca Rueth; Siede Preis Photography; Rémy Simard; Stockbyte; George Ulrich; Ted Williams.

Louis Weber, CEO
Publications International, Ltd.
7373 North Cicero Avenue
Lincolnwood, Illinois 60712

Permission is never granted for commercial purposes.

Manufactured in China.

8 7 6 5 4 3 2 1

ISBN-13: 978-1-4127-1182-1
ISBN-10: 1-4127-1182-7

Publications International, Ltd.

Contents

Get Ready to Read!

Why wait for school—give your preschooler every possible educational advantage now! Start your child down the exciting road to learning with this fantastic book. *My First 1000 Words* is a picture/word book that helps pre-readers understand the relationship between text and speech. Read along with your child, and watch the connections form. The vocabulary words are grouped according to categories children will recognize instantly.

Each word is paired with a vibrant image to help kids connect

words to people, places, and things around them.

Many categories also include sample sentences that show young readers the vocabulary words used in action. Several of these sentences contain *Dolch* sight words— common words

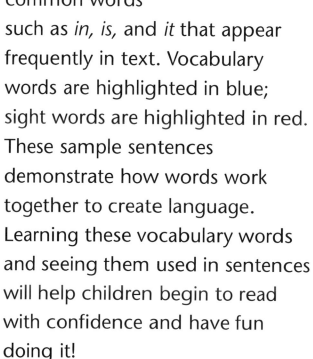

such as *in, is,* and *it* that appear frequently in text. Vocabulary words are highlighted in blue; sight words are highlighted in red. These sample sentences demonstrate how words work together to create language. Learning these vocabulary words and seeing them used in sentences will help children begin to read with confidence and have fun doing it!

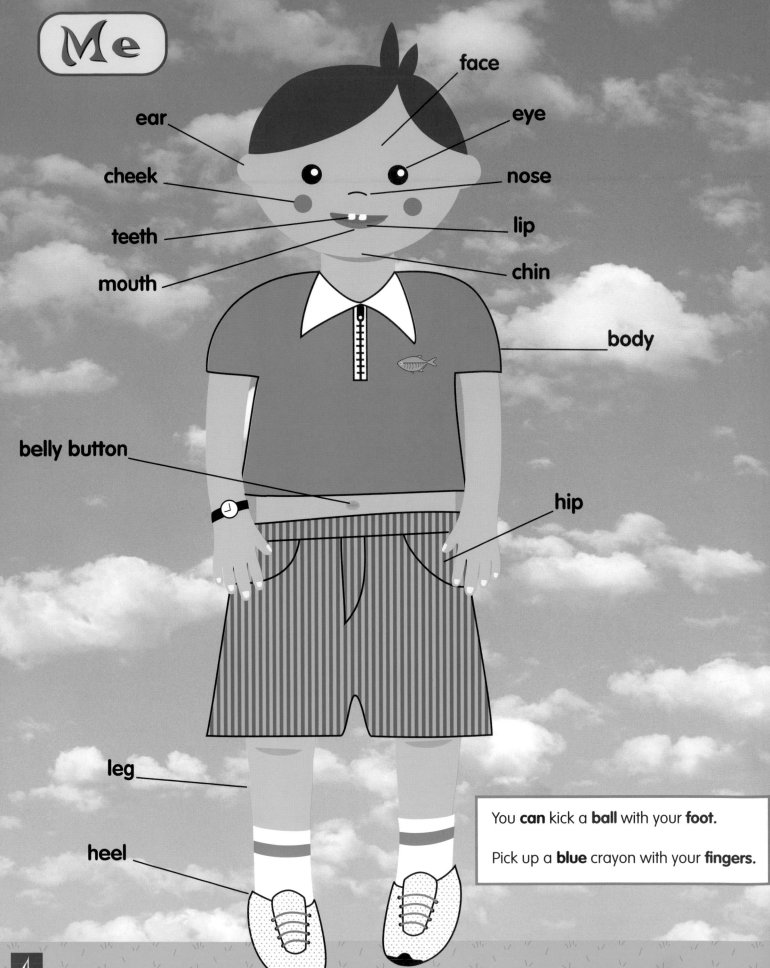

Me

face
ear
eye
cheek
nose
teeth
lip
mouth
chin

body

belly button

hip

leg

heel

You **can** kick a **ball** with your **foot**.

Pick up a **blue** crayon with your **fingers**.

4

head

hair

eyebrow

finger

forehead

hand

eyelashes

wrist

tongue

neck

elbow

shoulder

arm

back

fingernail

waist

knee

foot

ankle

toe

5

My Family

parents

father

mother

daughter

sister

brother

son

granddaughter

grandson

6

grandmother

grandfather

uncle

cousin

aunt

Clothes

When it rains, use an **umbrella** and wear a **raincoat** and **galoshes**.

The girl wore her **pretty bathing suit** to the beach.

sock

dress

hat

jeans

mittens

belt

glove

cap

bathing suit

vest

pajamas

shorts

skirt

shirt

apron

bonnet

underpants

jacket

snowpants

T-shirt

sunglasses

watch

zipper

button

scarf

necktie

sweater

umbrella

boots

shoes

sneakers

galoshes

flip-flops

slippers

9

My Home

chimney

house

roof

window

porch

door

welcome mat

garage

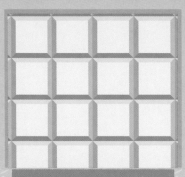

yard

driveway

fence

mailbox

gate

sidewalk

road

log cabin

hut

castle

apartment

mobile home

igloo

teepee

town house

The **king** and **queen** live in a **castle.**

The **yellow car** is parked in the **garage.**

The **roof** keeps the people **who** live in the **house** dry.

11

painting

lamp

vase

fireplace

sofa table

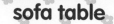

couch

floor

telephone

candle

coffee table

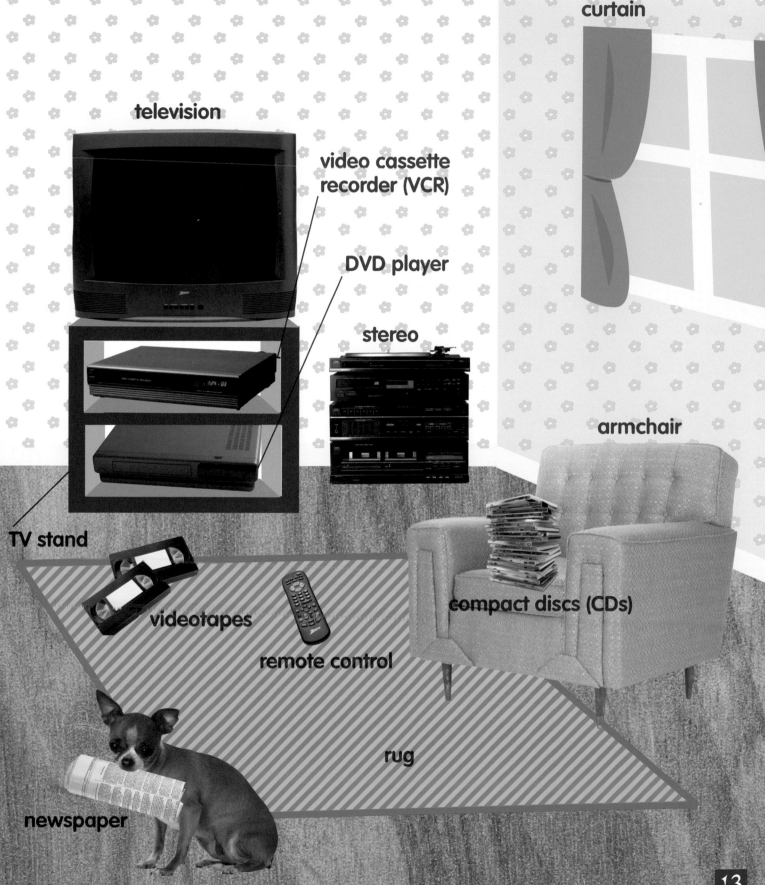

wall

curtain

television

video cassette recorder (VCR)

DVD player

stereo

armchair

TV stand

compact discs (CDs)

videotapes

remote control

rug

newspaper

Kitchen

refrigerator

salt   pepper

cupboard

cup

meal   blender   coffeemaker

bottle

dishwasher

glass

high chair

chair

14

pot

toaster

teapot

plate   dessert

microwave oven

drink

countertop

pan

kettle

stove

oven

straw

silverware

spoon

bowl

napkin

knife

fork

table

Water is boiling in the **kettle** on the **stove**.

One egg **is** cooking in the **pan**.

The **refrigerator** keeps the milk cold.

15

Bathroom

mirror

toothbrushes

lotion

hair dryer

comb

shampoo

toothpaste

soap

shower

washcloth

sink

faucet

tissue

towels

toilet

rubber duck

bathtub

Bedroom

frame

picture

shelf

closet

poster

peace

radio

drawer

dresser

wastebasket

clock

pillow

blanket

sheet

carpet

bed

nightstand

stuffed animal

All the **clothes** are hanging neatly **in** the **closet.**

His mother tells **him to** make the **bed.**

Garage and Laundry

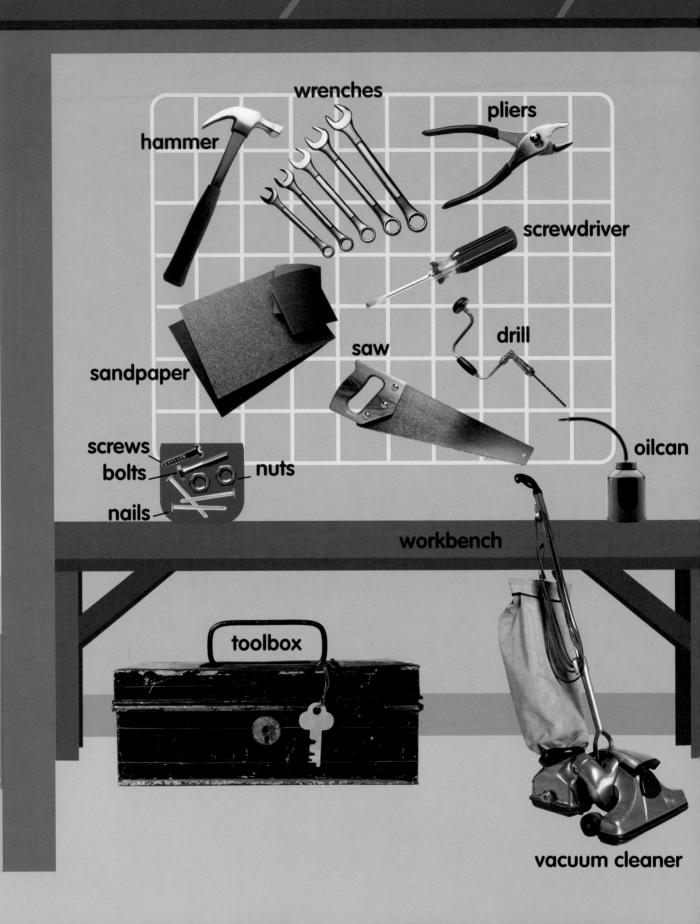

hammer

wrenches

pliers

screwdriver

sandpaper

saw

drill

oilcan

screws

bolts

nuts

nails

workbench

toolbox

vacuum cleaner

ironing board

plane

Pound the **nails** in the wood **with** a **hammer.**

Cut the **wood** with the **saw.**

Store the **nuts, bolts,** and **screws** in the **toolbox.**

iron

tape measure

washer **dryer**

detergent

SOAP

dustpan

broom

laundry basket

mop

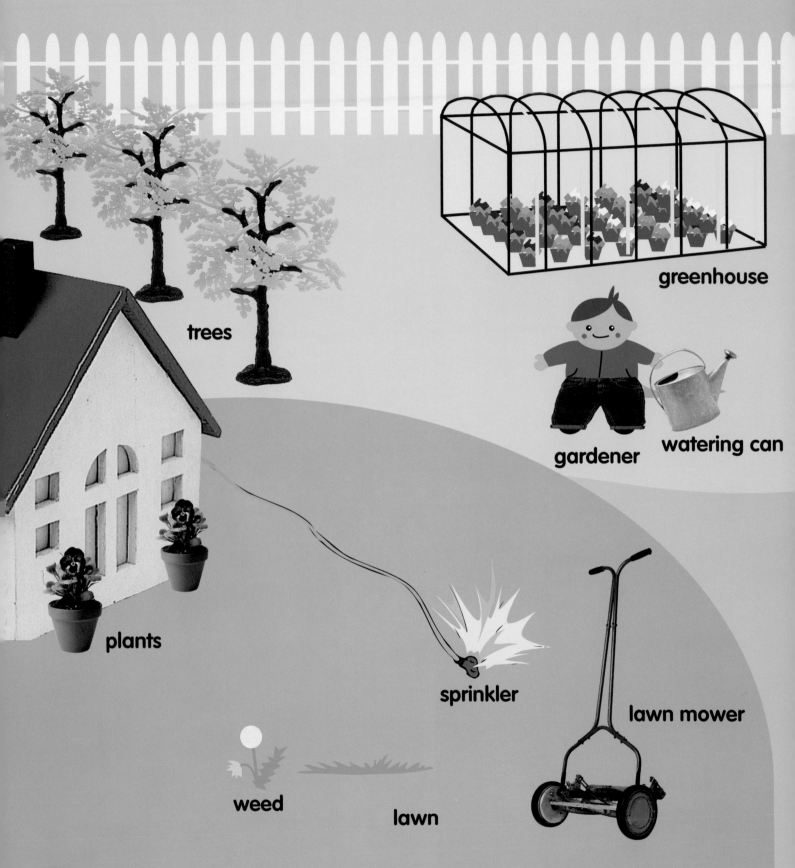

My Backyard

greenhouse

trees

gardener

watering can

plants

sprinkler

lawn mower

weed

lawn

20

shed

flowers

bush

wheelbarrow

dirt

shovel

rake

My School

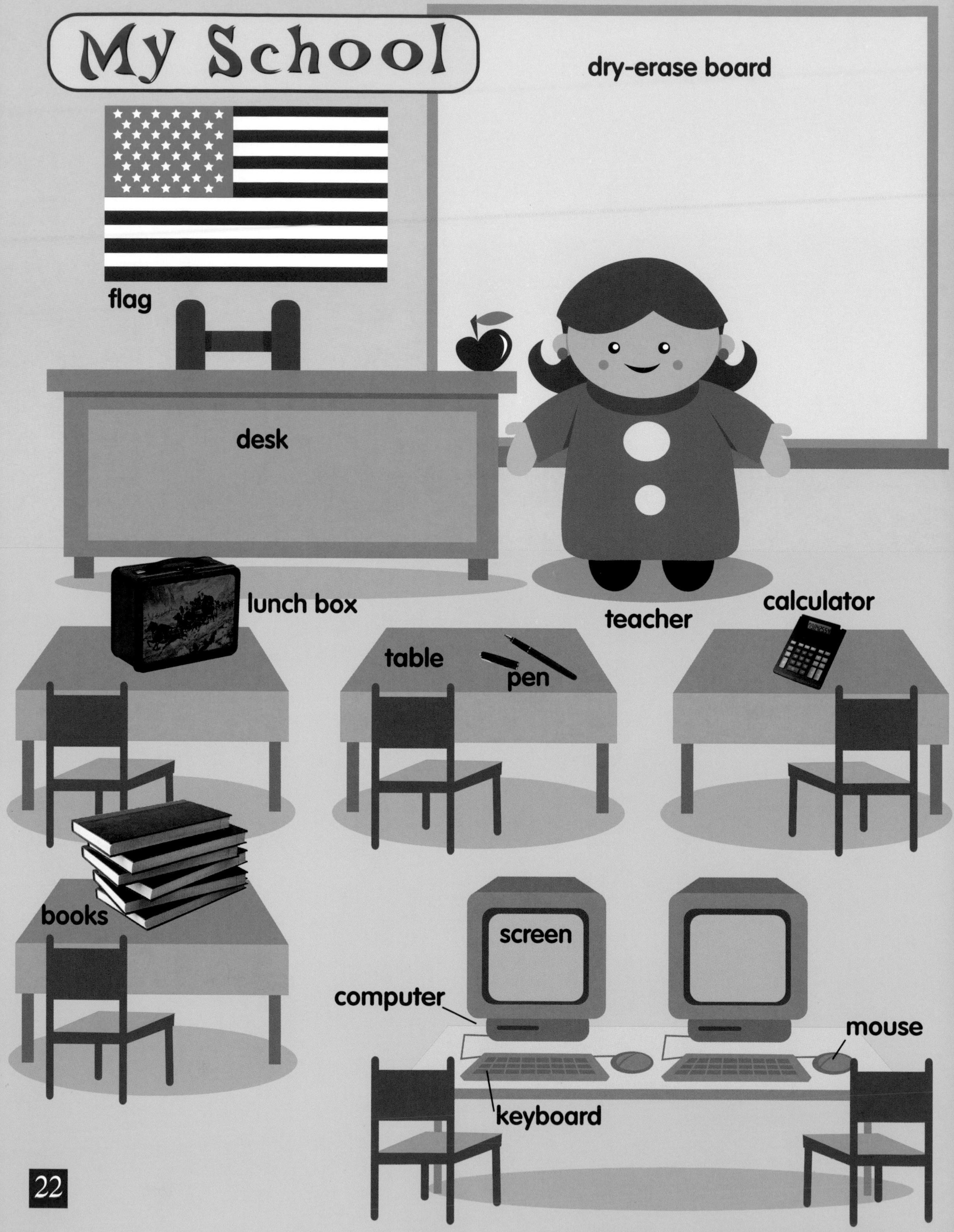

dry-erase board

flag

desk

teacher

calculator

lunch box

table

pen

books

screen

computer

mouse

keyboard

Three **friends** are reading **funny books** together at the **table**.

The **teacher** is writing on the **dry-erase board** with a **marker**.

microscope

globe

binders

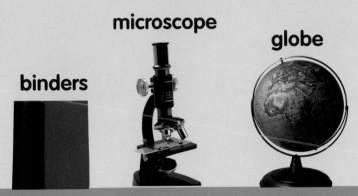

pencils

drawing

stool

paper

backpack   student

principal

23

Playground

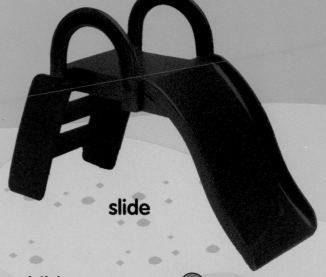

slide

swings

boy

children

merry-go-round

girl

jungle gym

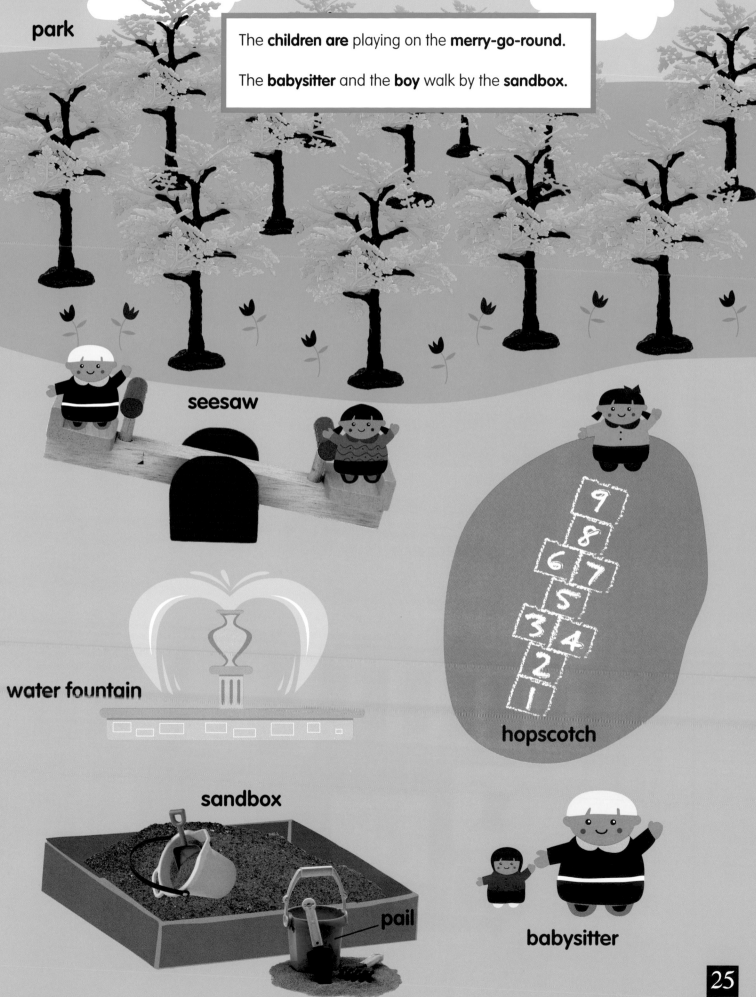

park

The **children are** playing on the **merry-go-round.**

The **babysitter** and the **boy** walk by the **sandbox.**

seesaw

water fountain

hopscotch

sandbox

pail

babysitter

25

Fire Station

fire pole

fire hydrant

alarm

fire extinguisher

helmet

mask

firefighter

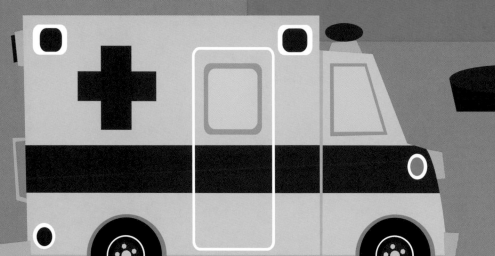

ambulance

ladder

hatchet

hose

fire truck

Police Station

POLICE

police car

uniform

badge

flashlight

motorcycle

POLICE

POLICE

police officer

27

My Doctor

A **patient** with a broken arm will need a **cast**.

The **nurse** takes a patient's temperature with **her thermometer**.

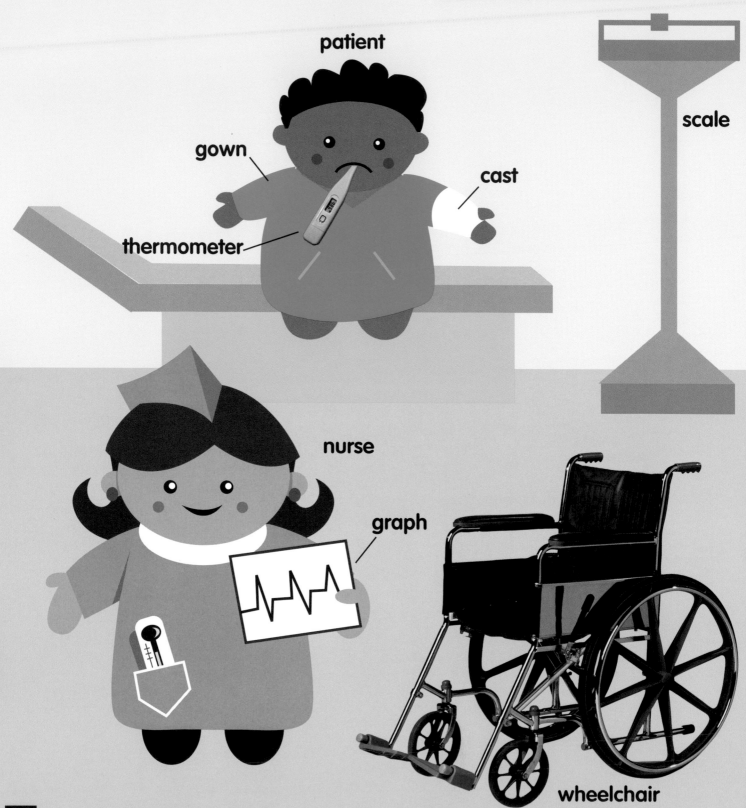

patient

gown

cast

scale

thermometer

nurse

graph

wheelchair

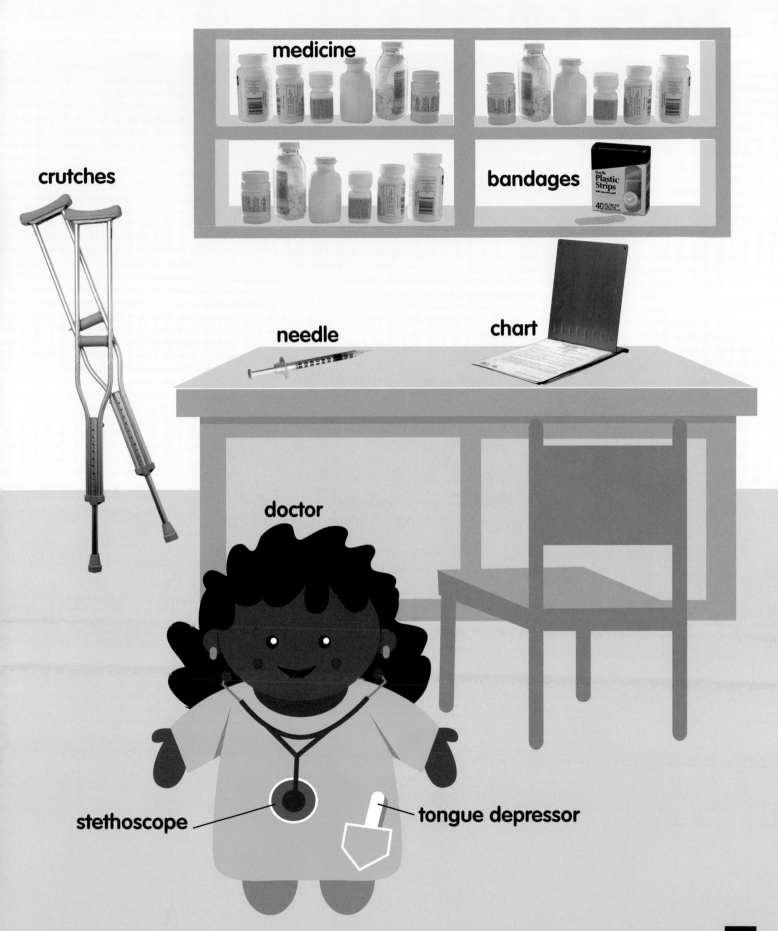

crutches

medicine

bandages

needle

chart

doctor

stethoscope

tongue depressor

29

Supermarket

jars

cans

watermelon

FREE SAVE

coupons

pineapples

noodles

CHILI BEANS

CHILI BEANS

CHILI BEANS

CHILI BEANS

CHILI BEANS

Vegetable Broth

Vegetable Broth

Vegetable Broth

Vegetable Broth

$1 OFF

SAVE

green beans

beets

Broth

Vegetable Broth

Vegetable Broth

Vegetable Broth

Vegetable Broth

carrots

celery

peppers

peas

vegetables

BAKERY

baker

pitas croissant English muffin

baguette

bread

bagels

butcher

meat

fish

steak ham

potatoes cabbage zucchini squash onions

grapes raspberries strawberries

fruit

cucumbers

corn blueberries cherries

31

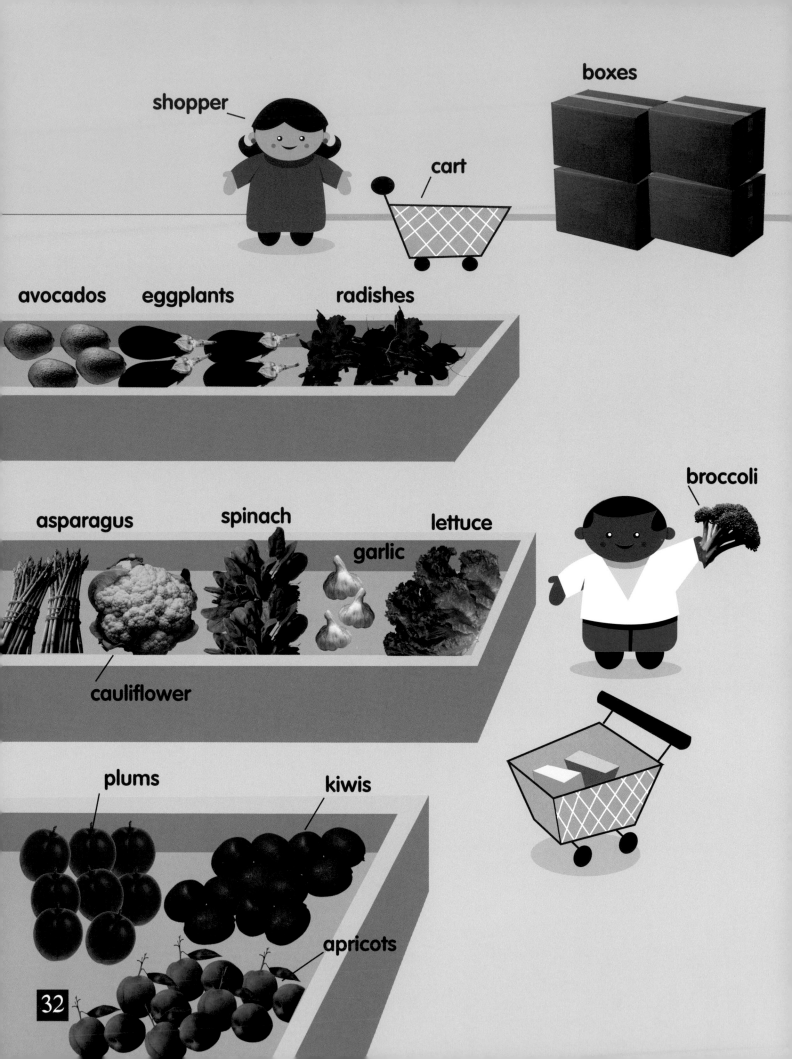

shopper

boxes

cart

avocados   eggplants   radishes

broccoli

asparagus   spinach   lettuce

garlic

cauliflower

plums   kiwis

apricots

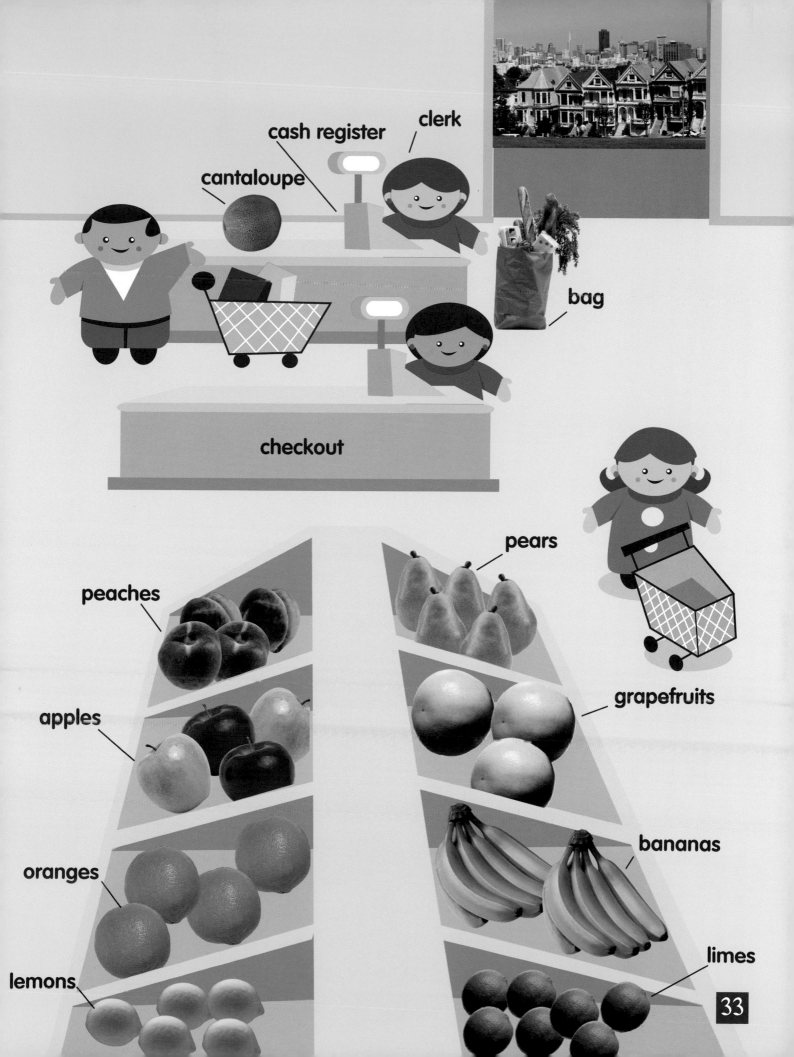

cash register

clerk

cantaloupe

bag

checkout

pears

peaches

apples

grapefruits

oranges

bananas

lemons

limes

33

Breakfast

sugar

honey

juice

tea

Maple Syrup

syrup

muffin

butter

egg

coffee

pancake

doughnut

jam

toast

bacon

sausage

cereal

Lunch

macaroni

milk

bun

hamburger

cheese

sandwich

hot dog

pickle

ketchup

tomato

mustard

roll

soup

Pancakes, bacon, and **sausage** are favorite **breakfast** foods.

Put **some ketchup** on the **hamburger.**

Dinner

spaghetti

rice

salad

chicken

pizza

water

Snacks and Dessert

yogurt

lollipop

popcorn

applesauce

cookie

ice cream

cupcake

raisins

gum balls

chips

crackers

pretzel

Popsicle™

chocolate

pie

Construction Site

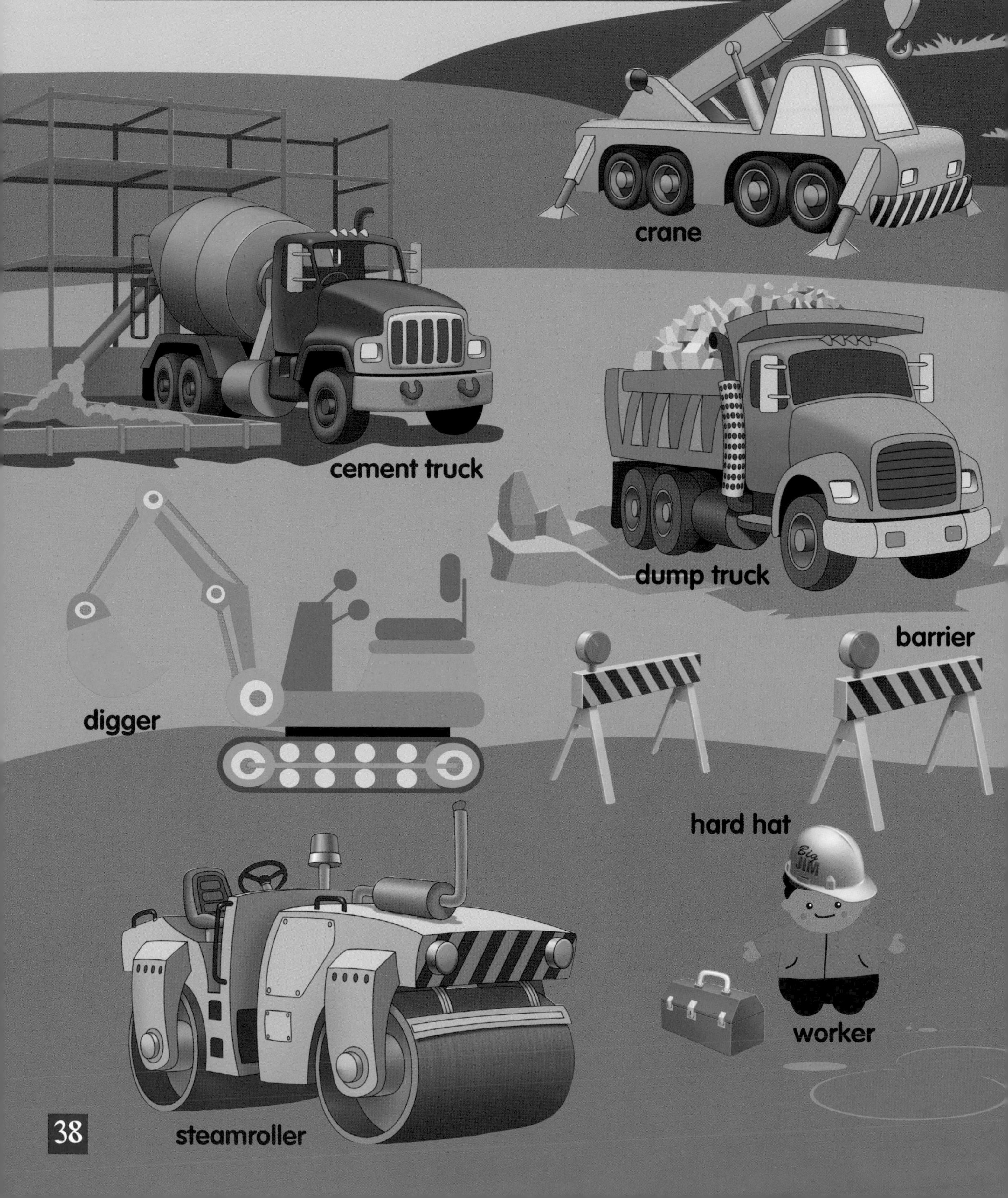

crane

cement truck

dump truck

digger

barrier

hard hat

steamroller

worker

backhoe

cone

bulldozer

forklift

bricklayer

bricks

grader

front loader

39

Park

kite

bench

picnic

trash can

cooler

grass

path

camera

man

woman

baby

stroller

40

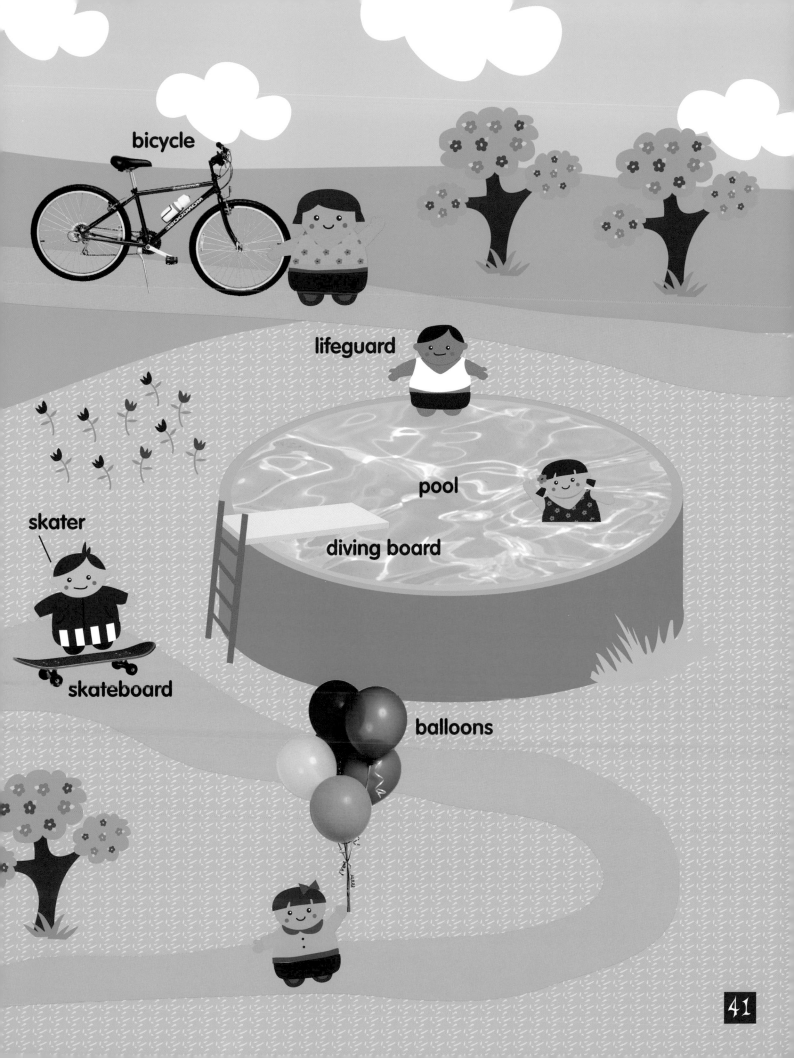

bicycle

lifeguard

pool

diving board

skater

skateboard

balloons

My Town

theater

SHOWTIME

Art Museum

LIBRARY

statue

church

synagogue

librarian

BANK

DRUGSTORE

Rx

POST OFFICE

laundromat

gas station

GARAGE

mechanic

GAS

CLEAN

KID CARE

$

MAIL

letter carrier

day care center

The man **ate** a sandwich **at** the **café** next to the **deli**.

The **bus** stops for the **traffic light by** the **bus stop**.

HOTEL

BUS STOP

NEWS

bus driver

newsstand

HOTEL

bus

traffic light

restaurant

department store

STORE

FLORIST

CAFÉ

DELI

DENTIST

salesperson

DINER

STOP

stop sign

At Work

clown

artist

coach

ballerina

mechanic

athlete

chef

server

housekeeper

44

movers

painter

musician

carpenter

scientist

pilot

manager

rose

sunflower

petal

leaves

thorn

stem

seeds

roots

daffodil

carnation

violet

daisy

iris

hyacinth

pansy

tulip

lily

cactus

lilac

orchid

47

Trees

pine tree

apple tree

pinecones

trunk

maple tree

48

palm tree

birch tree

coconut

oak tree

branch

bark

acorns

49

On the Farm

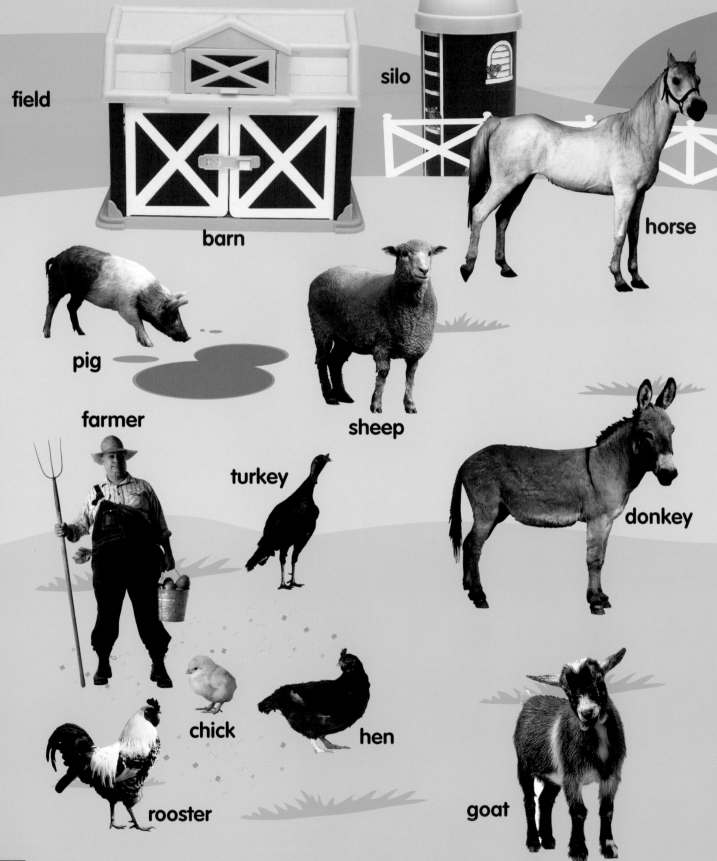

field

silo

horse

barn

pig

sheep

farmer

turkey

donkey

chick

hen

rooster

goat

tractor

farmhouse

hay

cow

well

wagon

goose

duck

duckling

pond

51

Pets

parakeet

parrot

cat

goldfish

snail

iguana

turtle

shell

rabbit

puppies

guinea pig

52

pony

kittens

dog

collar

leash

hamster

ferret

Wild Animals

cheetah

mane

lion

kangaroo

giraffe

quills

rhinoceros

porcupine

horns

alligator

tusks

elephant

bear

54

zebra

panda

fox

antlers

squirrel

wolf

deer

snake

monkey

skunk

raccoon

tiger

mouse

chipmunk

55

Ocean Animals

killer whale

jellyfish

fin

shark

gills

clown fish

octopus

tentacle

dolphin

seal

sea horses

fish

claw

lobster

starfish

Birds

nest

owl

swans

wing

robin

pigeon

feathers

penguin

flamingo

hummingbird

58

crow

blue jay

beak

eagle

dove

emu

peacock

Bugs and Insects

butterfly

moth

ladybugs

bee

ants

dragonfly

spider

web

fly

mosquito

caterpillar

cocoon

grasshopper

61

Transportation

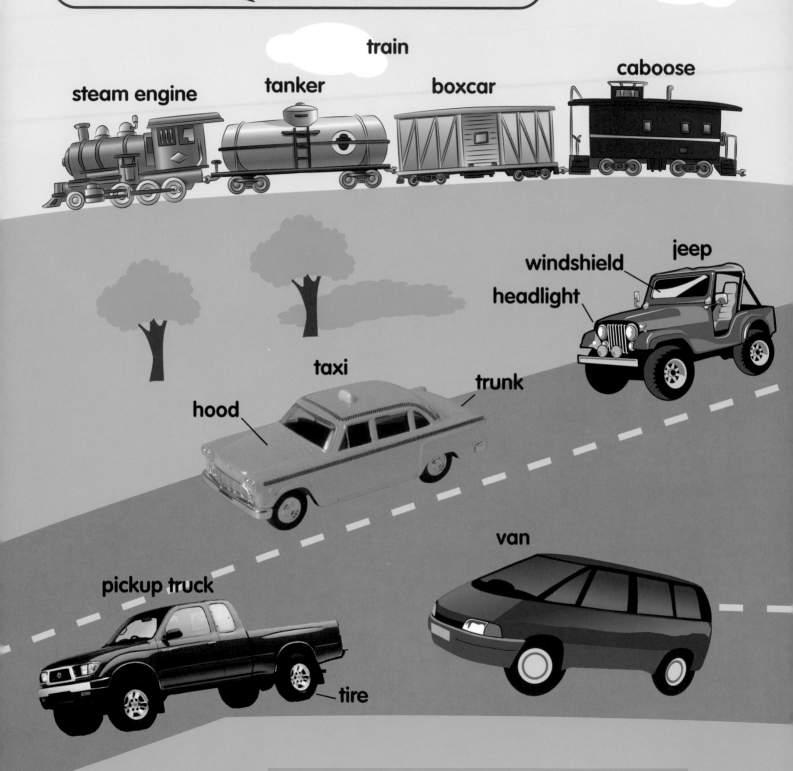

train

steam engine

tanker

boxcar

caboose

windshield

jeep

headlight

taxi

hood

trunk

van

pickup truck

tire

The top of the **red convertible** can go **up** and **down**.

People ride to the **airport** in **a taxi**.

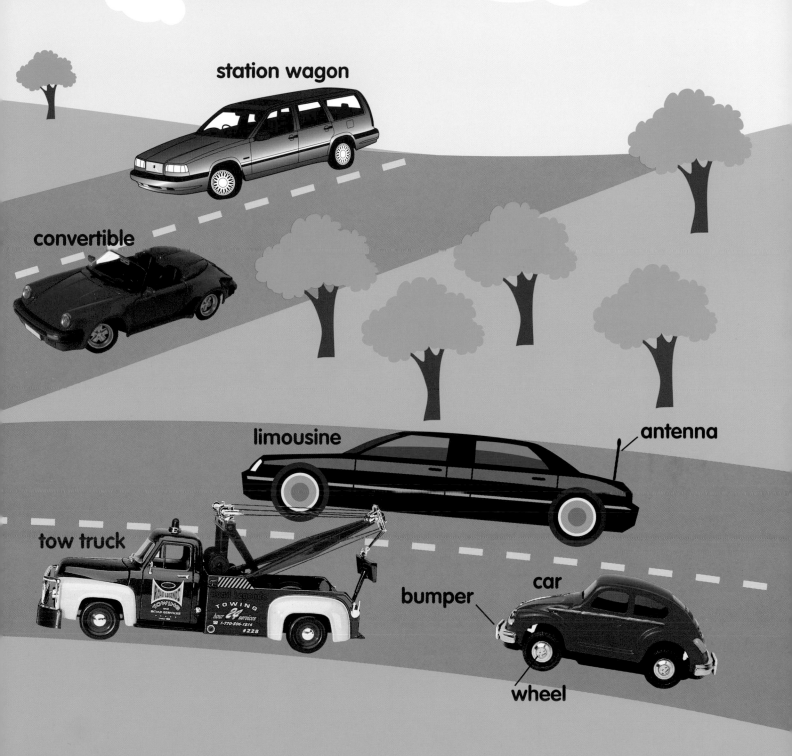

station wagon

convertible

limousine

antenna

tow truck

bumper

car

wheel

63

blimp

airplane

wing

hang glider

watercraft

rowboat

paddle

kayak

oar

speedboat

submarine

There is **one sailboat** on the lake one **raft** on the shore.

64

hot air balloon

helicopter

propeller

raft

canoe

yacht

anchor

ship

sailboat

Toys

The **teddy bear** is **brown**.

The **tricycle** is **new**.

The **beach ball** is **under** the **puppet**.

teddy bear

tea set

tricycle

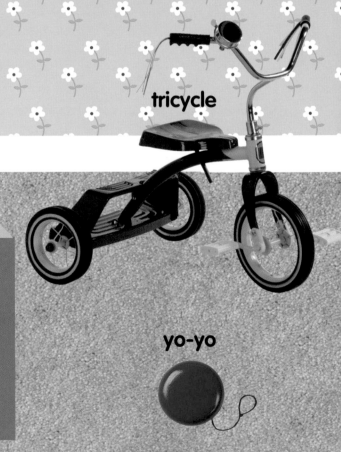

yo-yo

puppet

puzzle

doll

dinosaurs

truck

blocks

beach ball

roller skates

ice skates

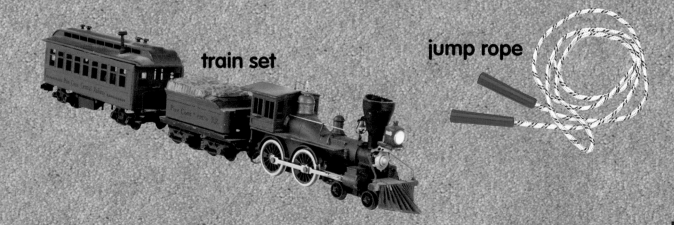

train set

jump rope

Costumes

knight

cowhand

fairy

wand

pirate

crown

angel

king

queen

cape

superhero

princess

prince

wizard

Statue of Liberty

genie

mermaid

69

Music

violin

flute

saxophone

oboe

xylophone

rhythm sticks

maracas

cymbal

drums

keyboard

The **top** of the **drum** is **round**.

The girl played the **saxophone again.**

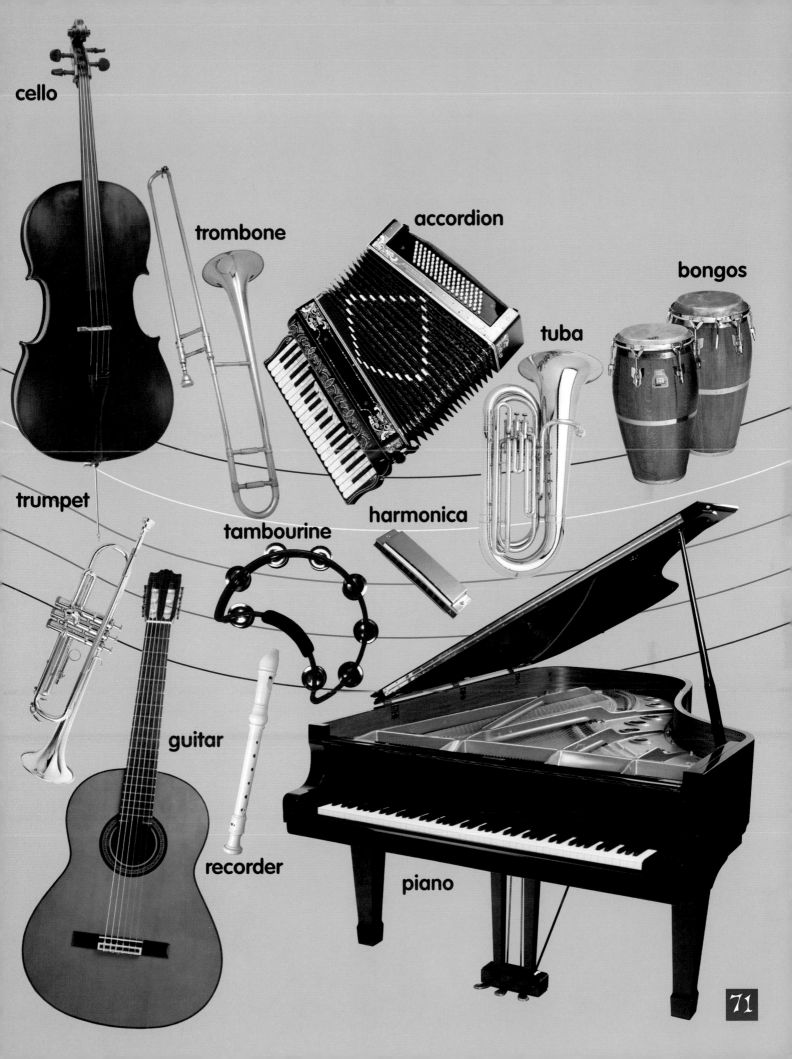

cello

trombone

accordion

bongos

tuba

trumpet

harmonica

tambourine

guitar

recorder

piano

71

crayons

clay

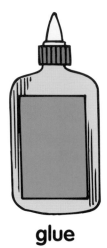

glue

markers

tape

paint

paintbrushes

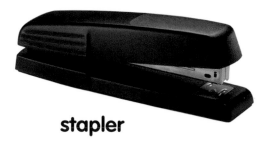

stapler

construction paper

eraser

scissors

ruler

colored pencils

easel

Sports

soccer

net

soccer ball

baseball

bat

goggles

swimming

flippers

hockey

hockey stick

ice-skating

puck

hockey skates

74

basketball

backboard

hoop

skiing

volleyball

volleyball net

poles

skis

racket

tennis

tennis ball

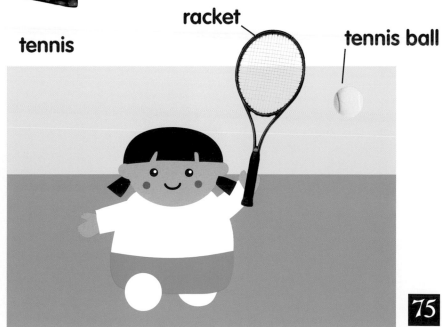

Hit the **tennis ball** with the **racket.**

Use the **flippers** to **go** fast when you are **swimming.**

The baseball player hits the **baseball** with his **bat.**

75

Solar System

astronaut

space shuttle

You can **see Saturn** by using a **telescope**.

Jupiter is the largest **planet** in **our** solar system.

Moon

Mars

Jupiter

Earth

Venus

Mercury

Sun

comet

76

planet

Pluto

Neptune

Uranus

Saturn

star

lens

tripod

telescope

Earth

forest

icebergs

waterfall

island   ocean

rain forest

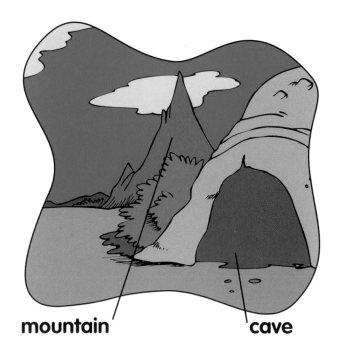

mountain   cave

river

lake

desert

volcano

swamp

beach

Seasons and Weather

spring

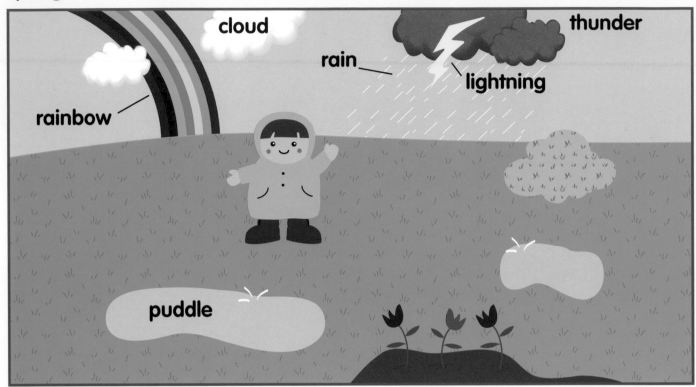

cloud

thunder

rain

lightning

rainbow

puddle

summer

sunny

sand

wave

fall

wind

hail

pile

winter

sleet

snow

ice

The **rainbow** has beautiful colors.

It is cold in **winter.**

When it **rains, there** are **puddles** on the ground.

Colors

blue

white

yellow

black

red

gray

orange

brown

purple

green

pink

Numbers

0 zero

1 one

2 two

3 three

4 four

5 five

6 six

7 seven

8 eight

9 nine

10 ten

11 eleven

12 twelve

13 thirteen

14 fourteen

15 fifteen

16 sixteen

17 seventeen

18 eighteen

19 nineteen

20 twenty

100 one hundred

1,000 one thousand

Money

 penny

 nickel

 dime

 **quarter**

dollar

wallet

piggy bank

purse

84

Shapes

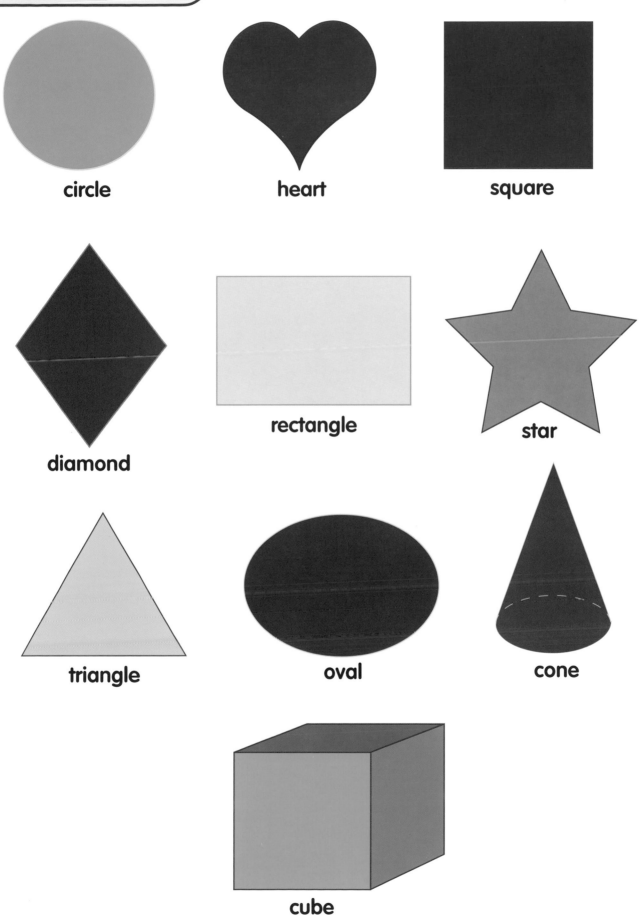

circle

heart

square

diamond

rectangle

star

triangle

oval

cone

cube

Action Words

carrying

building

walking

running

laughing
crying
crawling

sitting

shopping

biking

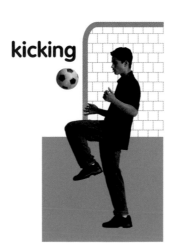
kicking

swimming

flying

singing

riding

washing

eating

dancing

reading

jumping

sleeping

playing

yawning

painting

87

Opposites

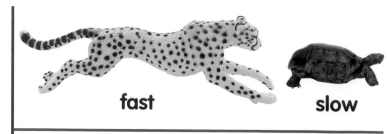

fast   slow

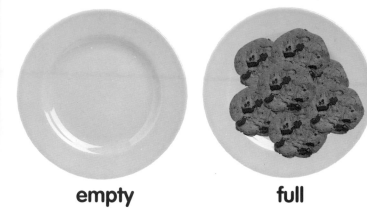

empty   full

old   new

wet   dry

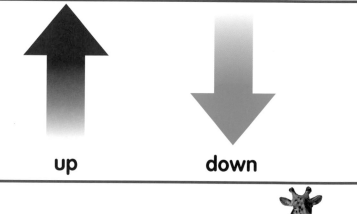

light   heavy

big   little

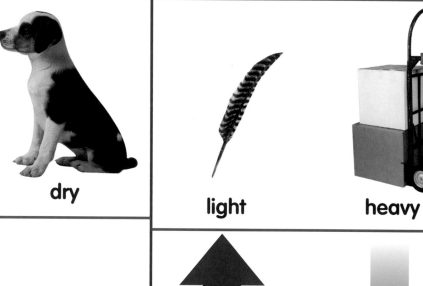

up   down

hot   cold

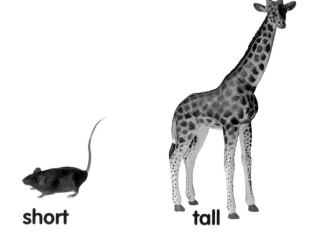

short   tall

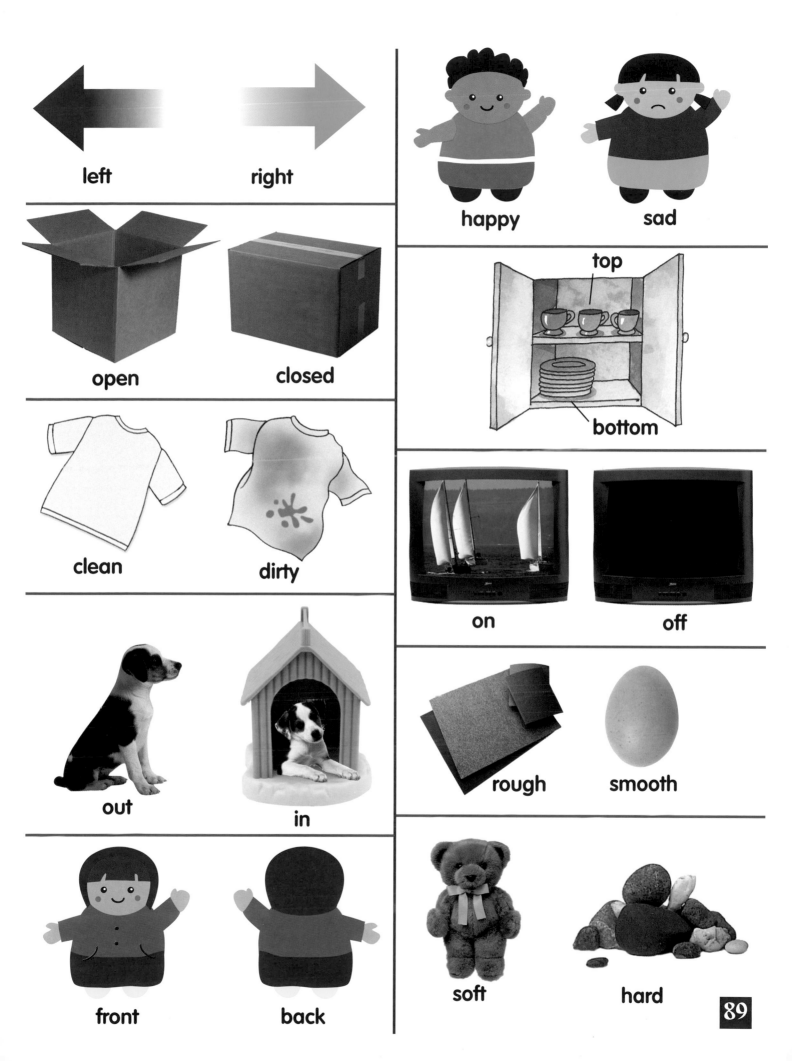

left

right

happy

sad

open

closed

top

bottom

clean

dirty

on

off

rough

smooth

out

in

front

back

soft

hard

89

Months and Days

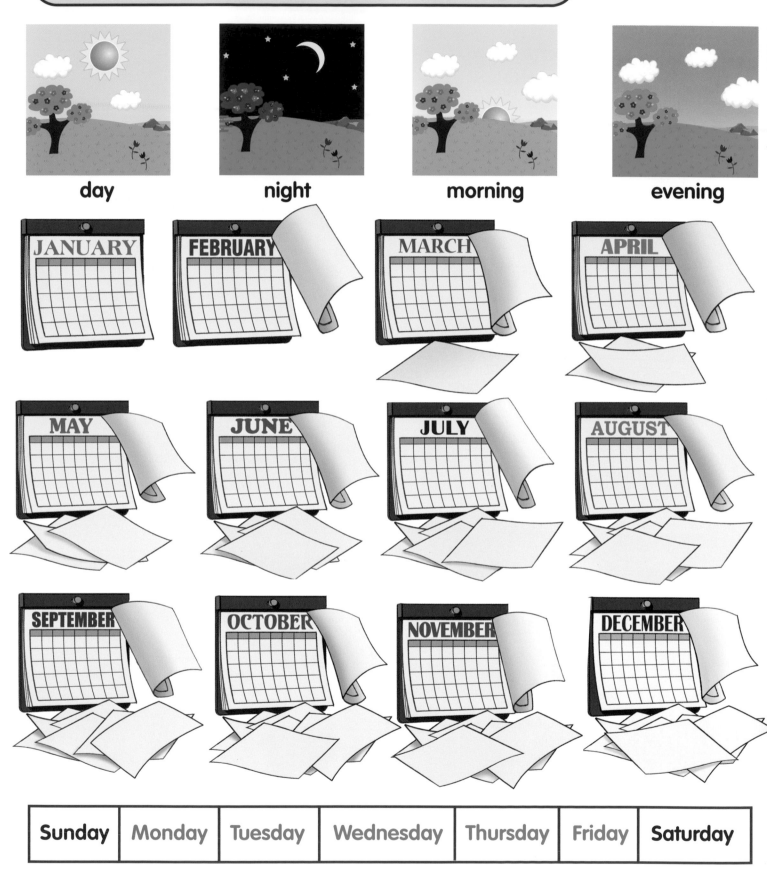

day　　　night　　　morning　　　evening

JANUARY FEBRUARY MARCH APRIL

MAY JUNE JULY AUGUST

SEPTEMBER OCTOBER NOVEMBER DECEMBER

Sunday	Monday	Tuesday	Wednesday	Thursday	Friday	Saturday

90

Holidays

Yom Kippur

Hanukkah

Independence Day

Christmas

Rosh Hashanah

Ramadan

New Year's Day

Passover

Columbus Day

Cinco de Mayo

St. Patrick's Day

Kwanzaa

Valentine's Day

Halloween

Presidents' Day

Memorial Day

Easter

Thanksgiving

91

Index